Into the Next Millennium

Engineering

Deborah Cannarella

Jane Fournier

The Rourke Press
Vero Beach, Florida

Photo credits

All images © copyright: AP/Wide World Photos, pp. 4 bottom and 18 middle, 19 bottom, 23 top and bottom, 25 top (Remy de la Mauviniere); Cameramann Int'l., Ltd., p. 19 top, 20 top; ChinaStock, p. 29 top (Christopher Liu); Corbis, pp. 10 top (Steve Kaufman), 10 bottom (Dean Conger), 14 top, 20 bottom (G. E. Kidder Smith), 21 top (Gail Mooney), 22 bottom (Roger Wood), 23 middle (Adam Woolfitt), 4 middle and 24 top (Bill Ross), 24 bottom (Roger Ressmeyer); 25 bottom (Tim Hawkins, Eye Ubiquitous); Corbis-Bettmann, pp. 8 bottom; Corbis/Historical Picture Archive, pp. 9 bottom, 14 bottom; Corbis/Hulton-Deutsch Collection, p. 15 top; Frank Gehry & Associates, p. 26–27 (Joshua White); Jeff Goldberg/Esto, p. 31 left; Mary Evans Picture Library, pp. 6 top, 13 bottom, 18 bottom; Massachusetts Turnpike Authority, p. 28; Mori Building Co., Ltd., pp. 27 top, 31 right; North Wind Picture Archives, pp. 6 bottom, 7 bottom; 8 top, 12 bottom, 15 bottom, 16 bottom, 4–5 and 17 top, 17 bottom; Reuters/ANSA/ Archive Photos, p. 29 bottom; Robert Fried Photography, p. 9 top; Solomon R. Guggenheim Foundation, p. 30 (David Heald); Stock Montage, Inc., pp. 1 and 22 top (David L. Brown); 4 top left and 7 top (Walker Collection), 11 top and bottom, 12 top, 13 top, 16 top, 18 top, 21 bottom. All cover and introduction page images PhotoDisc.

The authors thank Robert Richardson, P. E., for his advice on the manuscript.

An Editorial Directions Book
Book design and production by Criscola Design

Library of Congress Cataloging-in-Publication Data

Cannarella, Deborah
     Engineering / Deborah Cannarella, Jane Fournier.
     p. cm. — (Into the next millennium)
     Summary : Surveys the development of engineering and notable achievements in the field, including the Wall of Jericho, the works of Archimedes, Roman roads, and the Panama Canal.
     ISBN 1-57103-272-X
     1. Engineering—History Juvenile literature. [1. Engineering—History.] I. Fournier, Jane, 1955– . II. Title. III. Series.
     TA149.C36 1999
     620—dc21
                                                    99-30926
                                                      CIP

Introduction

The history of the human race is a story of great discoveries and amazing achievements. Since ancient times, people have found creative solutions to problems, met impossible challenges, and turned visions into reality. Each of these remarkable people—and each of their contributions—changed the world they lived in forever. Together, they created the world we know and live in today.

The six books in this series—*Medicine, Transportation, Communication, Exploration, Engineering,* and *Sports*—present a timeline of the great discoveries and inventions that have shaped our world. As you travel from ancient to modern times, you will discover the many ways in which people have worked to heal sickness, shape materials, share information, explore strange places, and achieve new goals. Although they worked with many different tools, their goal was always the same: to improve our quality of life.

As we enter the twenty-first century, we will continue to build on what each generation of people before us has created and discovered. With the knowledge they have given us, we will discover new ways to build, heal, communicate, discover, and achieve. We will continue to change the world in ways we can only begin to imagine.

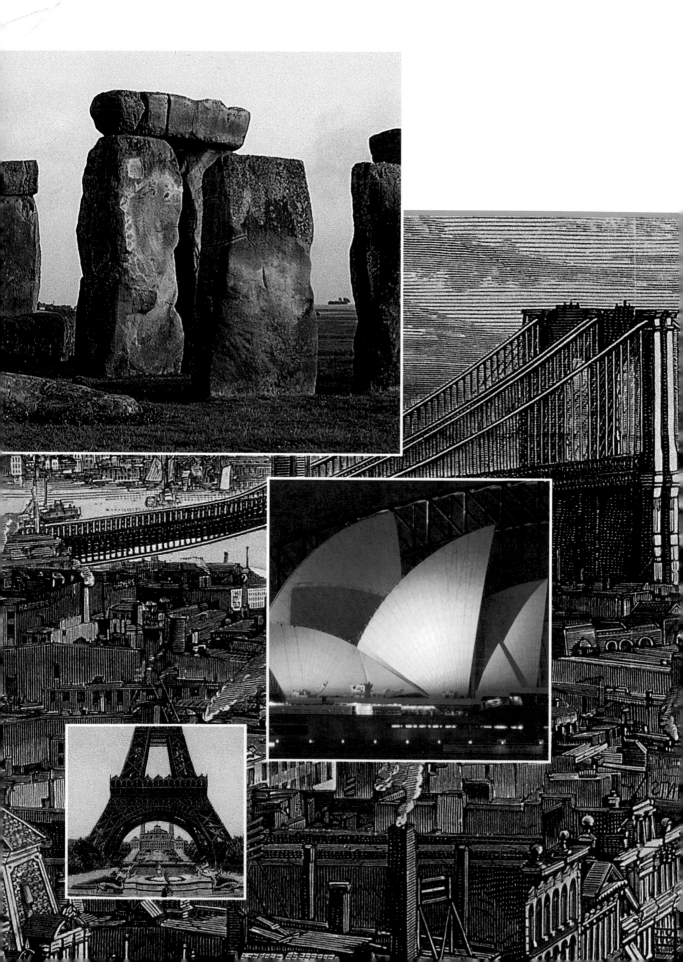

From the Past...

8000 B.C.

Jericho was one of the **first cities** in the world. By about 8000 B.C., the people had built a large stone wall, about 13 feet (4 m) high, around the city. There was also a lookout tower, about 28 feet (8 m) high. The wall and tower were built to protect the city from invaders. These were the first known structures to be built for defense. By about 1500 B.C., however, Jericho had been destroyed.

According to the Old Testament of the Bible, Jericho was attacked by Joshua in about 1200 B.C. The city's great wall was destroyed by the sounds of trumpets and shouting.

4000 B.C.

A **canal** is a man-made waterway. Ancient Egyptians built a canal around a waterfall on the Nile River in about 4000 B.C. Canals are built for travel and to route water from one place to another.

3000 B.C.

Stonehenge, located near Salisbury, England, is a circle of large, cut stones. Some historians believe that Stonehenge was a religious center. It is one of the earliest examples of a **post-and-lintel** building. One post, called a lintel, rests on two standing posts. This method of building is also found in ancient Greek and Roman temples.

Bricks—solid blocks of clay used for building—date from about 6,000 years ago. The bricks made by early people were dried by the Sun. Later, bricks were dried by fire in special ovens called kilns.

2500 B.C.

The **pyramids** of Egypt are among the Seven Wonders of the Ancient World. One of these huge structures—known as the Great Pyramid—contains more than 2 million stone blocks. Each block weighs more than 2 tons. Hundreds of thousands of builders dragged the blocks to the building site. They built dirt and brick ramps to move the blocks to each level of the pyramid. The Great Pyramid is 481 feet (147 m) high.

1300 B.C.

The Greeks built **underground tombs,** or burial places, out of stone. These structures were built as domes—round, curved structures shaped like an upside-down bowl. The tombs were about 43 feet (13 m) high and 47 feet (14 m) wide.

In the third century B.C., a stone lighthouse more than 350 feet (110 m) high—was built in Egypt. This lighthouse, called the Pharos, was the first "high-rise" building. Animals traveled on ramps to carry the fuel for the light at the top. The Pharos is one of the Seven Wonders of the Ancient World.

250 B.C.

The inventor Archimedes designed a tool for removing water that had gathered in the bottom of a ship. One end, which resembled a pipe with a screw inside, was placed in water. As the tool was turned, the water traveled up the pipe. The principle of this tool, which is called the **Archimedean screw,** is still used in some water pumps today. Archimedes also invented the pulley, a machine that made it possible to move great weight with only a small amount of force.

19 B.C.

The **Pont du Gard** is a large bridge and aqueduct over the Gard River in France. An aqueduct is a passageway designed to carry water. This aqueduct was built by the ancient Romans. The structure, which is made up of three levels of arches, is 155 feet (47 m) high.

The Romans invented a type of concrete similar to the building material used today. Their concrete, made with ash from volcanoes, made it possible for them to build their famous buildings, roads, and bridges—many of which still exist.

126

The ancient Roman building known as the **Pantheon** is the largest dome built in the ancient world. It is 142 feet (43 m) high and wide. Domed roofs do not require columns for support. They are supported by the outer walls of the building. The Pantheon, which was completed in the year 126, was built of brick and concrete. It still stands in Rome today in its original form.

200

In about 312 B.C., the ancient Romans began to build one of the first **systems of roads.** By the year A.D. 200, they had built 50,000 miles (80,000 km) of roads. These straight, solid roads were made of layers of stone with layers of lava blocks on top. The lava blocks formed a smooth, strong surface for traveling. The roads were 16 to 20 feet (5 to 6 m) wide. Roman roads continued to be used in the Middle Ages, and sections still exist today.

A windmill is a machine with blades or sails that are turned by the wind. The first windmills—built in about A.D. 600—were used to grind grain and water crops. By the 1400s, people in the Netherlands used windmills to drain water out of flooded lands.

214

The **Great Wall of China** is the longest structure ever built. The brick and dirt wall, which crosses northern China, was built entirely by hand. It is about 30 feet (9 m) high and 4,000 miles (6,400 km) long. Most of the wall was rebuilt during the period known as the Ming dynasty (1368 to 1644).

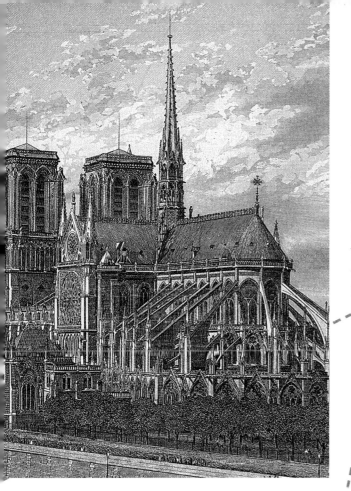

1175

A buttress is a brick or stone support on the outside wall of a building. A **flying buttress** is an arched support that extends, or "flies," from the wall to the ground. The famous Notre Dame Cathedral in Paris (left) was one of the first buildings with flying buttresses. These supports strengthened the walls, but also left enough free space for large stained-glass windows.

In the 1660s, scientist Sir Isaac Newton and philosopher Gottfried W. Leibniz each developed a mathematical system known as calculus. This system allows scientists and engineers to solve problems that involve curved areas, speed, and motion—which cannot be solved with other types of mathematics, such as algebra or geometry.

1442

A crane is a machine that lifts and moves heavy objects. Early cranes were powered by humans walking on a treadmill—steps attached to large moving wheels. This drawing of a **human-powered crane** is based on a carving found in ancient Rome. The oldest existing human-powered crane dates from 1442 in Gdansk, Poland. It was able to lift 4 tons and was used to load and unload ships.

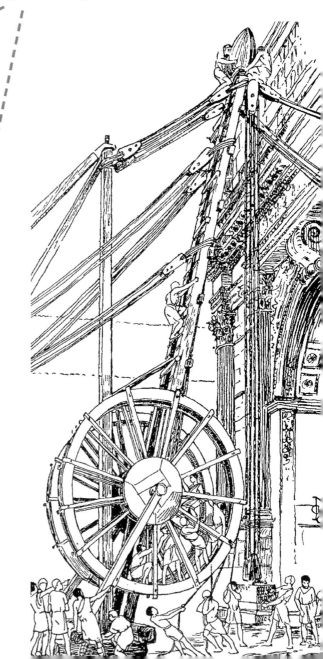

1632

The **Taj Mahal** in India was built by the emperor Shah Jahan as a tomb for his wife. It took more than 20,000 workers 22 years to built the monument. The white marble building stands on a platform of red sandstone. A prayer tower, 133 feet (41 m) high, stands at each corner of the platform. The dome in the center of the building is 120 feet (37 m) high and 70 feet (21 m) in diameter.

The first ironworks in America were established on the James River in Virginia in 1619.

1759

John Smeaton built a solid **stone lighthouse** in Eddystone, England. He arranged the blocks so that they locked together and would not collapse—as an earlier lighthouse had—under the pounding waves of the sea. Smeaton developed a mortar (a material used to join bricks and stones) made from a mixture of limestone and clay. His mortar worked well underwater and was an early version of the portland cement used today.

1779

The first **cast-iron bridge** was built by Abraham Darby in Coalbrookdale, England. Darby was the grandson of the ironmaker by the same name. Earlier bridges had been made of timber and stone or brick. The bridge, which was about 100 feet (31 m) long, was made of five arched ribs, cast in two halves. The bridge survived floods that destroyed the stone bridges in the area. Darby's arched bridge, called Ironbridge, is a British national monument.

1841

The first **underwater tunnel** was the Thames Tunnel, built under the River Thames in England. In 1818, designer Marc Brunel had invented the tunneling shield—a machine that digs in soft ground. Brunel got his idea by watching how a shipworm bore through wood. Before Brunel's invention, it had been impossible to build a tunnel underwater without the tunnel's collapsing. The Thames Tunnel, which was 1,506 feet (459 m) long, was completed in 1841. It is still used today as part of the London Underground railway system.

Between 1709 and 1713, Abraham Darby developed a process for making iron in furnaces fueled with a coal product known as coke. The quality of the iron produced with Darby's process made it possible to make cast (molded) iron for pots, steam engines, and even bridges.

1850

One of the earliest **railroad bridges** was the Britannia Bridge, built in Wales by engineer Robert Stephenson. His bridge was the first to use hollow, iron supports called box girders. The rectangular shape of the girders allowed large ships to sail underneath the bridge, without being blocked by the curve of arches.

The Crystal Palace was built in Hyde Park, London, for the Great Exhibition of 1851. More than 6 million people visited the nearly 14,000 exhibits, which included displays of false teeth, artificial legs, rubber goods, and tobacco.

1851

The Crystal Palace, a huge structure of glass and iron, was one of the first **prefabricated buildings**. A prefabricated building is assembled with parts that have been made at a factory. Crystal Palace, which was 1,851 feet (564 m) long, was built in only six months. Thin, iron rods support its great walls of clear glass. In 1936, most of the Crystal Palace was destroyed by fire.

1855

Engineer John Roebling was famous for his **steel suspension bridges.** The traveling surface of this type of bridge is suspended, or hangs from, cables. The cables are supported by two, high towers. Suspension bridges are usually built across long distances—especially, deep water or canyons—where it is difficult to build standing supports. Roebling built this railway bridge, which was 821 feet (250 m) long, across the Niagara River in New York.

Dynamite was developed by Alfred Nobel in 1867. The explosive's name is from the Greek word *dynamis*, which means "power." Dynamite was more powerful than black powder and safer than pure nitroglycerin—the blasting explosives used at the time.

In 1856, Sir Henry Bessemer developed the first method for manufacturing steel. His process involved a special furnace, known as a Bessemer converter.

1859

The first **oil well** was built in Titusville, Pennsylvania, by Edwin L. Drake. Drake's drill was powered by an old steam engine. The drill consisted of a sharp tool attached to a lever that raised the tool up and down, driving it deeper into the ground until it reached an underground source of oil. The well was a great success, and soon more wells were drilled nearby. By the early 1860s, this area of Pennsylvania had become a center of the oil industry.

1869

The **Suez Canal is** one of the most important canals in the world. It connects the Mediterranean and Red Seas, making a direct route between Europe and Asia. The canal is 105 miles (168 km) long. Before the canal was built, ships traveling from England to India had to travel 6,000 miles (9,700 km) more. The canal, which took 11 years to build, opened in 1869.

In 1964, the National Park Service designated the Brooklyn Bridge a national historic landmark.

1874

The Eads Bridge was the **first important steel bridge.** At the time, it was the largest bridge ever built. Its three arches, each about 500 feet (150 m), long spanned the Mississippi River in St. Louis, Missouri. Engineer James Buchanan Eads created a new system for building the arches. It was called the cantilevering method. While the bridge was being built, the arches were held up by cables supported by towers. The cables and towers were removed after the arches could support themselves.

1883

The **Brooklyn Bridge** crosses the East River in New York, connecting Brooklyn to Manhattan Island. This suspension bridge was designed by John Roebling, who also built the Niagara Bridge. The Brooklyn Bridge, which spans 1,595 feet (486 m), was the longest suspension bridge in the world at the time. It was also the first bridge built with steel cable wires. The cables are 16 inches (41 cm) thick. The bridge includes a six-lane roadway for automobiles and a broad walkway for pedestrians.

1885

William Le Baron Jenney designed the **first metal skyscraper.** The Home Insurance Building in Chicago, Illinois, was 10 stories high. The building was supported by a frame of iron and steel columns and beams. Instead of supporting the building, the walls hung on the frame. This new method of construction made buildings lighter, which made it possible to make them taller. The Home Insurance Building was torn down in 1931.

1889

Engineer Gustave Eiffel won a contest held by the French government. In only a few months, he built his iron tower for the Centennial Exposition in Paris. Until 1930, the **Eiffel Tower,** which was 984 feet (300 m) high, was the tallest building in the world. Gustave Eiffel became known as the Magician of Iron. He also designed the framework of the Statue of Liberty, a gift to the United States from France, which stands in New York Harbor.

Glass elevators travel along the curved arches of the base of the Eiffel Tower. The elevators were designed by the Otis Elevator Company. In 1854, Elisha Graves Otis had invented the safety hoist for passenger elevators.

1890

Workers began to build the tunnels for London's tube—the **first electric underground railway system**—in 1866. Engineer James Henry Greathead designed a tunneling shield to dig out the soft ground under the River Thames. In Greathead's system, compressed air behind the shield kept the tunnel from flooding. Modern tunneling shields are based on his design. The 3-mile (5-km) tube line opened in London in 1890. Today, the tube is the largest subway system in the world, with more than 100 miles (161 km) of rail lines.

1890

Benjamin Baker designed a **cantilever bridge** for railroad passage over the mouth of the River Forth in Scotland. In this type of construction, two beams, which are supported on one end, extend toward each other. A third beam spans the distance between them. The Forth Bridge has three, large cantilevered sections. A rocky island in the middle of the river supports one section. The steel bridge, which spans about 1 mile (1.6 km), was the longest bridge in the world at the time it was built.

One of the world's longest suspension bridges spans the River Forth at Queensferry, Scotland. It is 8,244 feet (2,513 meters) long and was completed in 1964.

1911

Walter Gropius was the founder of the **Bauhaus,** an art movement that joined art and design with craft and industry. His building designs combined simple forms and modern materials. His first large structure, the Fagus Works shoe factory, was built in 1911. The walls are almost entirely glass, with brick and steel supports. Here, Gropius stands in front of a drawing of the Chicago Tribune Tower, a design he produced with Adolf Meyer for a contest in 1922.

1914

The **Panama Canal** links the Atlantic and Pacific Oceans. The canal is about 51 miles (82 km) long. Engineers dug out about 211 million cubic yards (161 million cubic m) of earth and rock to build it. During 1913, more than 43,400 people worked on the canal. Water levels in the many locks are raised and lowered to allow ships to continue along the waterway. As shown here, the ships are towed into the locks by electric towing locomotives that travel along the sides.

Walter P. Chrysler, owner of the Chrysler Corporation—an automotive company—asked designer William Van Alen to add automobile designs to his office building. Stainless-steel images of radiator caps and hood ornaments can be found in some of the decorative work.

1930

For about one year, the **Chrysler Building** in New York City was the tallest building in the world. The skyscraper is 1,048 feet (319 m) tall and has 77 stories. Its famous shiny, stainless-steel spire is decorated with a pattern of sunbeam arches. The building's decoration and simple, geometric form make it a good example of the style of architecture and design known as Art Deco.

1931

In 1931, the **Empire State Building** became the world's tallest building—which it was for 24 years. The building has 102 stories. It was built in a series of steplike shapes called setbacks so that sunlight could reach the buildings and streets below. Its strong, steel framework is covered with panels of limestone and metal. Lookout decks on the 86th and 102nd floors provide visitors with spectacular views of the skyline of Manhattan. The Empire State Building is a good example of Art Deco design.

Photographer Lewis Hine was hired to take pictures during the building of the Empire State Building. To get the best photos, he shot from swinging baskets or buckets that hung hundreds of feet above the city streets.

1936

Dams have been built since ancient times to stop the flow of water. The **Hoover Dam,** on the Colorado River, is the largest concrete dam in the world today. Lake Mead, which is formed by the damming of the river, is the largest man-made lake in the world. Hoover Dam is 726 feet (221 m) high and 1,244 feet (379 m) long. The concrete base is 660 feet (200 m) thick. This powerful dam helps control flooding, produces electric power, and provides water for irrigation and other needs.

1937

The **Golden Gate Bridge** is one of the world's largest suspension bridges. It was designed by Joseph B. Strauss to connect northern California to the peninsula of San Francisco. The bridge is 8,981 feet (2,737 m) long. It has sidewalks and a six-lane road for traffic. The roadway hangs from two steel cables, 36 $\frac{1}{2}$ inches (93 cm) in diameter. The cables are connected to two towers, which are 4,200 feet (1,280 m) apart—one of the world's longest bridge spans.

In 1940, the Tacoma Narrows Bridge was twisted and destroyed by mild winds. Engineers discovered that the solid deck was not strong enough to resist the wind. The bridge was nicknamed Galloping Gertie. A new Tacoma Narrows Bridge, built in 1950 was designed with a stronger deck that allowed wind to pass through it.

1959

The **Solomon R. Guggenheim Museum** in New York City was designed by architect Frank Lloyd Wright. This white, concrete structure is built in the shape of a spiral. The six stories of the museum follow a ramp in the center of the building, from the floor almost to the ceiling. Light enters through a ceiling dome of glass. Wright designed the building with the idea that people would take the elevator to the top and view the artwork as they walked down the spiral ramp to the ground level.

1964

One of the longest suspension bridges in the United States is the **Verrazano-Narrows Bridge,** built by Othmar H. Ammann. It connects Brooklyn to Staten Island across New York Harbor. The main span is 4,260 feet (1,298 m). It has a double-deck, six-lane highway. The roadway is supported by four cables—weighing almost 10,000 tons each—that are attached to towers 690 feet (210 m) high.

During the building of the Golden Gate Bridge, engineers and workers struggled with many problems—frequent storms and fog, rapid waters, and the difficulties of blasting rock underwater to build strong foundations that could withstand earthquakes.

1970

The **World Trade Center,** which includes six office buildings, is a business center in New York City. Two of its buildings are twin towers. Each tower is 1,350 feet (411 m) tall, with 110 stories and 21,800 windows. Until 1974, these buildings, designed by Minoru Yamasaki, were the tallest buildings in the world.

1973

Jørn Utzon's first design for the **Sydney Opera House** in Australia was impossible to build. He changed the design slightly, but the building still presented many engineering problems. The white, curved, concrete roofs resemble the sails of a ship. They are covered with more than 1 million small, ceramic tiles, each about 5 inches (13 cm) square. To attach the tiles, workers had to climb up the curved roofs with ropes. They worked sitting in small chairs, wearing safety belts. The building took more than seven years to build.

The Petronas Twin Towers were built in Malaysia in 1996. They are 1,482 feet (452 m) tall with 88 stories. The towers are connected by a skybridge.

A French engineer first had the idea for an underwater tunnel from England to France in 1802. In 1882, the British began to drill with the first tunnel-boring machine, which dug at the rate of only about 50 feet (15 m) a day. They stopped after only 8,000 feet (2,400 m), fearing their enemies would use the tunnel for attack.

1974

In 1974, the **Sears Tower,** an office building in Chicago, Illinois, became the tallest skyscraper in the world. The building is 1,454 feet (443 m) tall and has 110 stories. The building was designed by Fazlur Khan for Sears, Roebuck and Company. Almost all of the welded steel parts of the frame were prefabricated. The frame was then bolted together during construction. The building has three setbacks, the first one at the 50th floor.

1976

The **Georges Pompidou Arts Center** was designed by Renzo Piano and Richard Rodgers of England. The outside of the building is covered with red, blue, and green pipes and structural supports. The tube-shaped escalators are also on the outside of the building. This unusual design creates the effect of a transparent, "inside-out" building.

To dig the Channel Tunnel, 11 huge tunneling machines—each longer than two football fields—removed about 10 million cubic yards (8 million cubic m) of the chalk that lies in the seabed. It took four years to dig the tunnel.

1994

The digging of the **Channel Tunnel,** also known as the Eurotunnel or Chunnel, began in 1987. The tunnel contains three tubes. Two provide rail service for goods and passengers. The third is used for maintenance and as a source of fresh air. The Channel Tunnel is 31 miles (50 km) long—23 $1/2$ miles (38 km) of it are about 130 feet (40 m) underwater.

...Into the **Future**

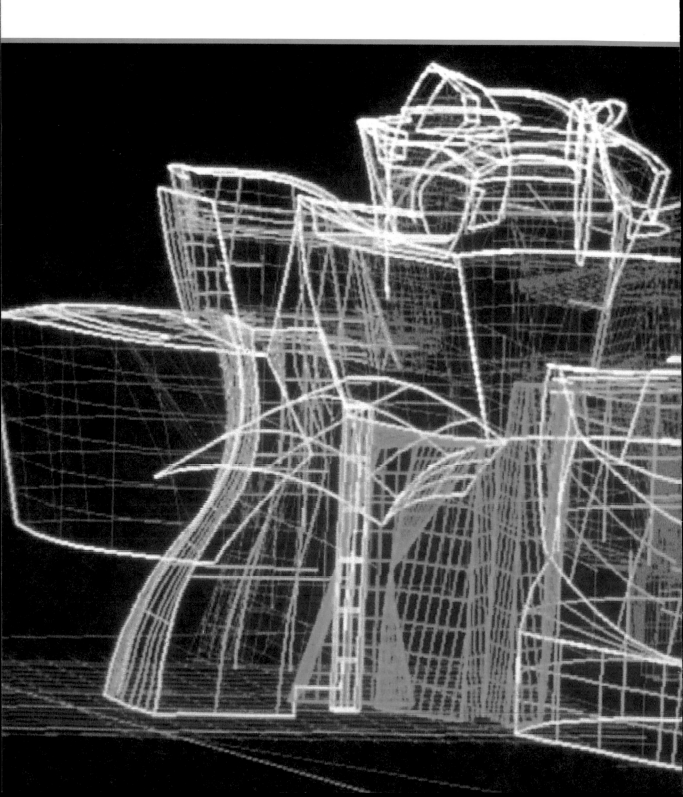

The Big Dig.
Engineers have designed a way to
solve the traffic problems in Boston,
Massachusetts, by 2004. The Big Dig will
replace a crumbling, 6-lane freeway with almost
8 miles (12 k) of a 10-lane underground highway
and a 14-lane bridge over the Charles River.
Underground highways can improve traffic flow
in crowded city areas. Engineers in Japan are
also designing new systems—including
underwater tunnels—to solve
traffic problems.

Giant dam.
The Three Gorges Dam on the Yangtze River in China will be completed in 2009. It will be the largest hydroelectric (water-powered electricity) plant in the world. The dam will be more than 600 feet (182 m) tall and 5,250 feet (1,600 m) long. It will produce electric power, control flooding, and make it easier for boats to travel along the river.

New materials will allow buildings to change their shape, stiffness, and strength to adapt to changing conditions—such as earthquakes, wind storms, and explosions. This "smart" matter will rely on sensors and computer processors. For example, when sensors in a building register an earthquake, they would send electrical signals to the building's shock absorbers. The "smart" shock absorbers will become stiffer, reducing damage to the building and its occupants.

Saving Venice.
Engineers are finding ways to protect the ancient city of Venice, Italy, from sinking. As sea levels rise and more land is covered by water, the city may be flooded completely by 2100. One plan is to place large, hinged barriers at the mouths of the city's three harbors. When the tidal waters reach flood levels, the barriers will keep water from rushing into the city.

Computer-aided design.
Frank Gehry designed the Guggenheim Museum Bilboa (above), which opened in Spain in 1997. He worked with Catia, a program that creates three-dimensional models on a computer screen. Catia also was used to make the building's full-size parts. Engineers and architects will continue to rely on computer-aided design (CAD) and computer-aided manufacturing (CAM) systems. CAM systems can direct the movements of the tools and even instruct robots.

An immersed-tube tunnel is built on land. The concrete sections are lowered to the seabed, joined with waterproof seals, and pumped dry. Immersed tunnels may be used to build a second Chunnel for automobile traffic and a roadway between Denmark and Sweden. Engineers are also designing tube tunnels—for cars, bicycles, and pedestrians—that would float about 82 feet (25 m) below the surface of the water.

Supertall buildings.
Supertall buildings—taller than the Petronas Twin Towers (left) and the Shanghai World Financial Center (right)—will appear in several cities around the world. Some will be more than 2,000 feet (610 m) tall. These hotels, offices, and apartment buildings will house thousands of people. To withstand winds and to support their weight—and the weight and traffic of the people inside—these structures will be designed and built with the most advanced engineering technology.

Computers and high-tech electronics will make houses and offices more "user-friendly." People will wear pins that will allow built-in sensors to follow their movements. Computers will open doors, turn on lights, and even change the artwork on the walls, to meet each person's needs.

Index

For further reading

Books

Cox, Reg, and Neil Morris. Illustrations by James Field. *The Seven Wonders of the Modern World.* The Wonders of the World series. New York: Silver Burdett Press, 1996.

Oxlade, Chris. Illustrations by Raymond Turvey. Photographs by Martyn Chillmaid. *Bridges and Tunnels.* Technology Crafts Topics series. Danbury, Conn.: Franklin Watts, 1994.

Parker, Jane, and Michael Pollard. Illustrated by Kevin W. Maddison. *Pyramids and Temples.* Austin, Tex.: Raintree/Steck-Vaughn, 1997.

Stone, Tanya Lee. *America's Top 10 Construction Wonders.* America's Top 10 series. Woodbridge, Conn.: Blackbirch Marketing, 1998.

Web sites

National Aeronautics and Space Administration
To access information on the International Space Station
http://station.nasa.gov/index-m.html

NOVA Online
To find out about different types of bridges and how they're built
http://www.pbs.org/wgbh/nova/bridge